GETTING TO KNOW THE WORLD'S GREATEST ARTISTS

J A C K S O N
POLLOCK

WRITTEN AND ILLUSTRATED BY MIKE VENEZIA

CONSULTANT MEG MOSS

CHILDRENS PRESS®

CHICAGO

*For the many future great artists and authors
at P.S. 111 in Manhattan. Keep up the good work!*

Cover: *Composition with Pouring II,* By Jackson Pollock. 1943. Oil on
canvas, 25 ⅛ x 22 ⅛ inches. Hirshhorn Museum and Sculpture
Garden, Smithsonian Institution, Washington, D.C. Gift of Joseph H.
Hirshhorn, 1966. © 1994 The Pollock-Krasner Foundation/ARS, New
York. Photographed by Lee Stalsworth.

Project Editor: Shari Joffe
Photo Researcher: Jan Izzo

Library of Congress Cataloging-in-Publication Data

Venezia, Mike.
    Jackson Pollock/written and illustrated by Mike
Venezia; consultant: Meg Moss
        p.   cm.–(Getting to know the world's greatest
artists)
    ISBN 0-516-42298-7
    1.   Pollock, Jackson, 1912-1956–Criticism and
interpretation–Juvenile literature.   2.   Abstract
expressionism–United States–Juvenile literature.
[1.   Pollock, Jackson, 1912-1956.   2.   Artists.
3.   Painting, American.   4.   Painting Modern–United
States. 5 Art appreciation.]   I.   Pollock, Jackson, 1912-
1956.II.   Title.   III Series: Venezia, Mike. Getting to
know the world's greatest artists.
ND237.P73V46 1992
759.13–dc20   93-36699
                                                          CIP
                                                          AC

Printed in China

19 20 21 22 R 10 09 08   62

Jackson Pollock
at work, 1950.
Photograph
© Hans Namuth,
1989.
Hans Namuth
Ltd., New York.

Jackson Pollock was born in Cody, Wyoming, in 1912. He was the youngest of five brothers, and grew up to be one of the greatest artists of the twentieth century.

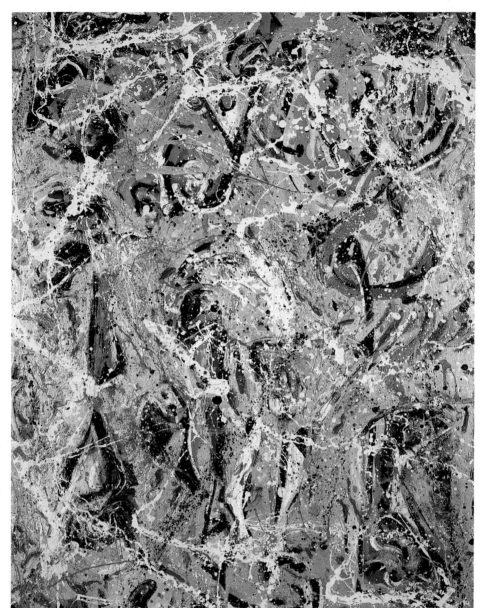

Galaxy, by Jackson Pollock. 1947. Oil and aluminum paint on canvas, 43 ½ x 34 inches. Joslyn Art Museum, Omaha, Nebraska. Gift of Miss Peggy Guggenheim. © 1994 The Pollock-Krasner Foundation/ARS, New York.

Jackson is best known for the huge paintings he made by splattering, throwing, and dripping paint onto his canvases.

Jackson used old, hardened
brushes, sticks, and anything else he
could find that would splatter on
paint the way he liked.

Jackson's style of art is often called Abstract Expressionism. Because Jackson moved around a lot and used so much energy while he painted, he preferred to call his style Action Painting.

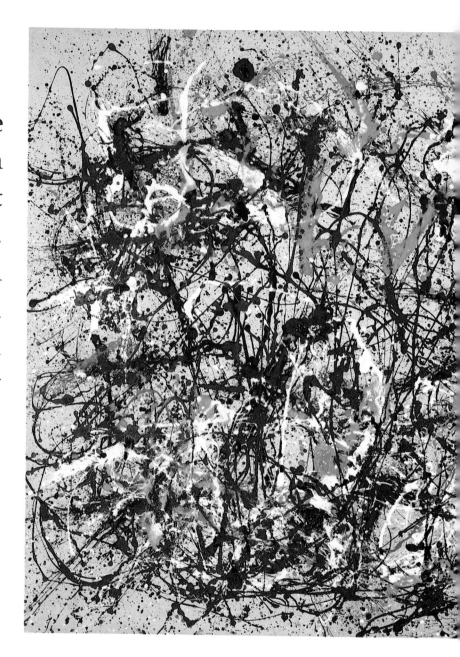

Autumn Rhythm, by Jackson Pollock. 1950.
Oil on canvas, 105 x 207 inches.
The Metropolitan Museum of Art, New York, New York.
George A. Hearn Fund, 1957.
Photograph © 1980, The Metropolitan Museum of Art.
© 1994 The Pollock-Krasner Foundation/ARS, New York.

Mural, by Jackson Pollock. 1943. Oil on canvas, 238 x 97¼ inches.
The University of Iowa Museum of Art, Iowa City, Iowa. Gift of Peggy Guggenheim.
© 1994 The Pollock-Krasner Foundation/ARS, New York.

Jackson Pollock wanted people to
feel and see the energy he felt while
painting. Even though you can't

recognize any objects in Jackson's most
famous paintings, they are filled with
expression, movement, and rhythm.

While Jackson was growing up, his
family moved all over the western
states, usually from one ranch or farm
to another. No matter how much work
needed to be done, Mrs. Pollock always

preferred to see her sons working on anything having to do with art. It was probably because of her encouragement that three of Jackson's older brothers also became artists.

When Jackson was eight years
old, his family moved to Janesville,
California. Many American Indians
lived in the area. Sometimes Jackson
and his brothers would sneak up into
the mountains to the Indian burial
grounds and watch their ceremonial
dances.

Bird,
by Jackson
Pollock. 1941.
Oil and sand
on canvas,
27 ¾ x 24 ¼
inches.
The Museum of
Modern Art,
New York. Gift
of Lee Krasner
in memory of
Jackson Pollock.
© 1994 The
Pollock-Krasner
Foundation/ARS,
New York.
Photograph
© 1993 The
Museum of
Modern Art,
New York.

An Indian woman who helped take care of Jackson and his brothers often told them Indian legends and stories. Years later, Jackson put mythological Indian creatures and symbols into some of his paintings.

When Jackson Pollock was just beginning high school in California, his oldest brother, Charles, was studying to be an artist in New York City. Charles often sent Jackson art magazines and wrote him letters about what he was learning. Jackson always admired his older brother's talent.

When Jackson was eighteen, his brother Charles returned home for a visit. When it was time for Charles to

return to New York, Jackson went
with him. He had decided to become
a serious artist, too.

When Jackson got to New York,
he entered the same art school that
Charles was going to, and had the
same teacher, Thomas Hart Benton.

Arts of the West, by Thomas Hart Benton. 1932.
Tempera with oil glaze, 96 x 156 inches.
New Britain Museum of American Art, Connecticut.
Harriet Russell Stanley Fund.

Thomas Hart Benton was already a famous American artist at that time. He was known for his large murals. A mural is a huge painting made to cover a wall or ceiling of a building. Jackson assisted Thomas Benton on some of his murals by posing, mixing paints, and cleaning the studio.

Jackson learned how large paintings were made, and tried to make his paintings look like Thomas Benton's. But Jackson had a difficult time giving his paintings the feeling and finished look he thought Thomas Benton would like.

Jackson Pollock always seemed to have trouble drawing things, too. No matter how hard he tried to make his drawings look the way he wanted, he just couldn't. It was almost like his hand and pencil refused to do what he wanted them to do.

Self Portrait, by Jackson Pollock. 1930. Oil on gesso ground on canvas, mounted on composition board, 7 1/4 x 5 1/4 inches. Courtesy Jason McCoy, Inc. © 1994 The Pollock-Krasner Foundation/ARS, New York.

Jackson often became angry and upset, but teachers kept working with him, because they knew how much he wanted to be an artist. The dark, gloomy look Jackson gave himself in the painting above might show how frustrated he felt.

One day, Jackson joined the workshop of a famous Mexican mural painter. David Siqueiros and his friends were experimenting with new types of paint and different ways of painting. They mixed oil colors with paint used for cars. They poured their colorful mixtures onto large canvases and spray-painted different surfaces just to see what would happen. Jackson was surprised. He noticed that beautiful and interesting shapes were being created.

Jackson thought that what he was
learning at Siqueiros' workshop might
help him create his own artwork
without having to draw perfectly.

During this time, Jackson learned all he could from the artwork of other modern artists whose paintings were shown at museums and galleries all over New York.

Jackson loved the mysterious, frightening, dreamlike scenes José Orozco painted in his murals. The strong, powerful shapes and symbols Pablo Picasso used reminded Jackson of American Indian art, and brought back memories from his past.

*The Epic of
American
Civilization,*
Panel #17:
*Gods of the Modern
World,* by José
Clemente Orozco.
1932-34. Fresco.
Commissioned by
the Trustees of
Dartmouth College,
Hanover,
New Hampshire.

Guernica, by Pablo Picasso. 1937. Oil on canvas, 138 x 308 inches.
Museum del Prado, Madrid, Spain.
Giraudon/Art Resource, New York.
© 1994 ARS, New York/SPADEM, Paris, France.

Male and Female,
by Jackson Pollock.
1942. Oil on canvas,
73 x 49 inches.
Philadelphia
Museum of Art,
Pennsylvania.
Gift of Mr. and Mrs.
H. Gates Lloyd.
© 1994 The
Pollock-Krasner
Foundation/ARS,
New York.

Stenographic Figure, by Jackson Pollock. 1942. Oil on linen, 40 x 56 inches.
The Museum of Modern Art, New York. Mr. and Mrs. Walter Bareiss Fund.
© 1994 The Pollock-Krasner Foundation/ARS, New York.
Photograph © 1993 The Museum of Modern Art, New York.

Jackson started to combine all the things he had learned with shapes and symbols from his own imagination. Soon his paintings started to look very different from anything he'd done before. He was finally developing his own way of painting, and people began to notice his brightly colored work.

Jackson kept using his imagination and began to create paintings that were *really* different. Symbols and shapes started to disappear, and his

Blue Poles, by Jackson Pollock. 1952. Oil, enamel and aluminum paint, glass on canvas, 83 x 185 5/8 inches. Collection of National Gallery of Australia, Canberra.
© 1994 The Pollock-Krasner Foundation/ARS, New York.

works became larger. He started to drip and splatter paint all over his canvas as a way to show his feelings.

In 1945, Jackson bought a farmhouse and married his girlfriend, Lee Krasner. Lee was an artist, too. She used one of the bedrooms of their house for a studio, and Jackson used the barn.

Jackson usually tacked his canvas
to the barn floor. He liked to walk all
around and be *in* his painting while
he worked. This way, Jackson felt that
he was really part of his work.

Jackson Pollock died in a car accident in 1956 when he was only forty-four years old. Even though he became famous during his life, he was often very unhappy.

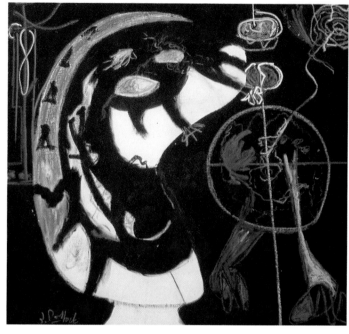

Night Sounds, by Jackson Pollock. 1944.
Oil and pastel on canvas, 43 x 46 inches. Private Collection.
© 1994 The Pollock-Krasner Foundation/ARS, New York.

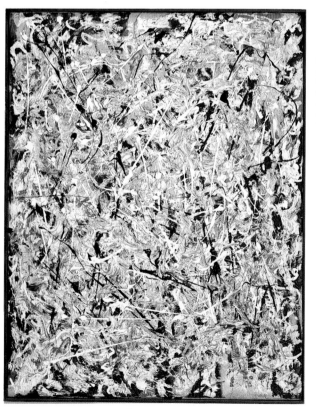

White Light, by Jackson Pollock. 1954.
Oil, enamel, and aluminum paint on canvas,
48 ¼ x 38 ¼ inches.
The Museum of Modern Art, New York.
The Sidney and Harriet Janis Collection.
© 1994 The Pollock-Krasner Foundation/ARS, New York.
Photograph © 1993 The Museum of Modern Art, New York.

Important people from all over the world loved to talk and write and argue about his exciting new paintings, but hardly anyone bought his work until years later.

Sometimes people have trouble understanding Jackson Pollock's paintings. They feel that anyone could have thrown paint around and done just as good a job. But Jackson knew exactly what he was doing. When you stand in front of a huge Jackson Pollock painting, you can get a feeling of being surrounded by light and color, movement and energy, that is very exciting!

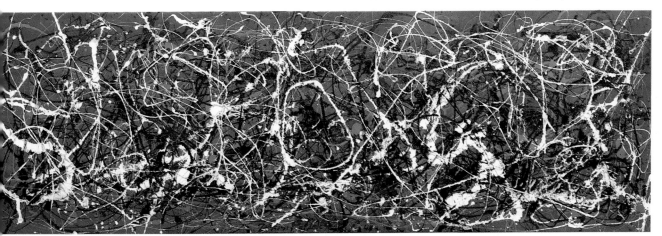

It's a good idea to see Jackson Pollock's paintings in person. The special feeling you get of being in an explosion of color and energy has a lot to do with their large size. The metallic and other different types of paint Jackson used help add to that feeling, too.

Detail of *Composition with Pouring II*

The paintings in this book came from:
Baker Library, Dartmouth College, Hanover, New Hampshire
Hirshhorn Museum and Sculpture Garden, Smithsonian Institution, Washington, D.C.
Joslyn Art Museum, Omaha, Nebraska
The Metropolitan Museum of Art, New York, New York
Museum del Prado, Madrid, Spain
The Museum of Modern Art, New York, New York
National Gallery of Australia, Canberra, Australia
National Museum of American Art, Washington, D.C.
New Britain Museum of American Art, New Britain, Connecticut
Philadelphia Museum of Art, Philadelphia, Pennsylvania
The University of Iowa Museum of Art, Iowa City, Iowa
Yale University Art Gallery, New Haven, Connecticut